Grammar Coach

Grammatik-Übungsheft für das 5. Schuljahr

Erarbeitet von:

Robert Klimmt
Jutta Stahl-Klimmt

Diesterweg
westermann

Bildquellen:

|Getty Images, München: CORBIS Royalty-Free Collection Titel.

Druck A[10] / Jahr 2024
Alle Drucke der Serie A sind im Unterricht parallel verwendbar.

Redaktion: André Schmitt
Illustrationen: Ulf Marckwort, Kassel
Umschlaggestaltung: Sandra Grünberg
Druck und Bindung: Westermann Druck GmbH, Georg-Westermann-Allee 66, 38104 Braunschweig

ISBN 978-3-425-**72151**-4

Inhalt

Vorwort

Liebe Schülerin, lieber Schüler,

wer eine fremde Sprache lernt, will andere Menschen verstehen können und von ihnen verstanden werden. Im Unterricht lernst Du nach und nach verschiedene sprachliche „Werkzeuge" kennen, mit deren Hilfe Du Dich in der Fremdsprache verständlich machen kannst. Zu diesen Werkzeugen zählt auch das Beherrschen von grammatischen Strukturen.

Wie man mit einem Werkzeug umgeht, lernt man am besten, indem man es benutzt. Dabei hilft Dir der *Grammar Coach*. Mit ihm kannst Du die Verwendung von grammatischen Strukturen einüben und wiederholen.

Du kannst mit dem *Grammar Coach* selbstständig zuhause arbeiten. Falls Du nicht sicher bist, in welchen Bereichen Du noch Übung benötigst, wird Dir Dein/e Lehrer/in sicherlich gerne Hinweise geben.

Die Übungen im *Grammar Coach* sind nach Grammatikpensen geordnet. Zum Beispiel findest Du die Übungsaufgaben zum *simple present* auf den Seiten 22–27. Bei den Pensen stehen jeweils zuerst die einfachen Aufgaben, dann folgen die schwierigeren.

Die anspruchsvollsten Übungen sind am linken Rand mit einer Sonne gekennzeichnet.

Die Lösungen findest Du am Ende des Heftes, so dass Du Dich selbst überprüfen kannst.

Viel Erfolg mit Deinem *Grammar Coach!*

Nouns: singular and plural (1)

Write down the plural forms of the words.
Schreibe die Mehrzahl der Wörter auf.

Example:  animal – *animals* 

1. shoe – ______________________
2. sausage – ______________________
3. watch – ______________________
4. day – ______________________
5. tooth – ______________________
6. hobby – ______________________
7. pet – ______________________
8. man – ______________________

Nouns: singular and plural (2)

Fill in the plural forms of the marked words.
Trage die Mehrzahl der markierten Wörter ein.

Example:  Tina has got one cat, but Tim has got five *cats*. 

1. A pirate has got one golden earring. My sister has got two pink ______________________.
2. This is not a good story. I like ______________________ about animals.
3. There is no glass on the table, but there are four ______________________ on the shelf.
4. We have got one shelf in the kitchen and two ______________________ in the living room.
5. We have all got one life, only cats have nine ______________________.
6. Flamingos can stand on one foot. We normally stand on two ______________________.

Nouns: singular and plural; "there is"/"there are"

Describe the picture.
Use "there is"/"there are".
Beschreibe das Bild.
Verwende „there is"/„there are".

Example: *There are two cars.*

____

____

____

____

____

____

____

____

____

____

The article

Add "a" or "an". *Ergänze „a" oder „an".*

Example: Silvia eats *an* ice cream.

1. Mrs Kent drives _____ green car.
2. My father has got _____ orange bike.
3. We live in _____ nice little street.
4. That's _____ interesting book.
5. Can you give me _____ apple, please?
6. Murat has got _____ uncle in Manchester and _____ aunt in Birmingham.

Personal pronouns (1)

Sort the words into the lists. *Ordne die Wörter in die Listen ein.*

he	she	it	they
	Caroline		

Example: Caroline 

1. a poster 

2. Mr Rice 

3. Emma 

4. a football 

5. a little dog 

6. CDs 

7. a boy 

8. a fish 

9. David and Hoover 

10. Grandma Simpson 

11. a cat 

12. friends 

Personal pronouns (2)

Put in the right word. *Setze das richtige Wort ein.*

~~It~~ • they • it • They • He • it • They • We • It • She • He • you • it

Example: This is the classroom. ____It____ is very big.

1. My friends and I are at the same school. __________ are in class 6b.
2. Our teacher is very nice. __________ doesn't give us very much homework.
3. My dream classroom has got sofas and laptops. And __________ has got a fridge for cold drinks.
4. "Where is Gillian?" – "__________ is not here."
5. Can you help me with this exercise? I don't understand __________.
6. Are you the new pupil? Where are __________ from?
7. I don't know this word. Can you spell __________?
8. Where are my sandwiches? __________ are not in my sandwich box.
9. "What's the time, please?" – "__________'s five o'clock."
10. "Do you like your classmates?" – "Yes, __________ are very nice."
11. Where is Rajiv? __________ is not in the classroom.
12. Rajiv and Charlie are good friends. __________ play together after school.

Personal pronouns (3)

Fill in the right personal pronoun.
Trage das richtige Personalpronomen ein.

The forgotten homework

___It___ is Friday. Mr Graham comes into the classroom.

__________ (1) talks and the children listen. __________ (2) all work hard, but Rajiv is not interested. __________ (3) loves English. But __________ (4) doesn't like numbers. __________ (5) are so boring. And __________ (6) can't understand them. Rajiv starts to dream about Caroline. __________ (7) is a very nice girl. __________ (8) is fun to be with her.

David's birthday party is this Saturday. David likes music and __________ (9) has got a lot of good CDs. Perhaps Rajiv can dance with Caroline at David's party. __________ (10) is a very good dancer.

"Rajiv, __________ (11) are dreaming in class. Sorry to wake __________ (12) up", says Mr Graham. Rajiv's face goes red. __________ (13) looks like a tomato. "Rajiv, where is your homework? Can __________ (14) see __________ (15)?" – "Oh, I'm sorry, __________ (16) haven't got it. __________ (17) is at home on my desk", says Rajiv. The bell rings. __________ (18) is five past three. All the pupils jump up. __________ (19) can go home now. But not Rajiv. __________ (20) talks to Mr Graham. The teacher says: "Rajiv, __________ (21) don't work hard. And __________ (22) forget your homework." – "Yes, Mr Graham. Can __________ (23) go to my friends now? __________ (24) are playing football in the park."

"Rajiv, do __________ (25) like Caroline? And does __________ (26) like you?" – "__________ (27) don't know", says Rajiv. __________ (28) is very red in his face.

"__________ (29) is OK", says Mr Graham. "__________ (30) can go. Have a nice weekend. And don't forget your homework on Monday." – "Thank __________ (31), Mr Graham. I won't forget __________ (32)."

The modal verb "can" (1)

Are the sentences true or false?
Stimmen die Sätze oder stimmen sie nicht?

	true (+)	false (-)
Example: A fish can live in water.	+	
1. Elephants can play the guitar.		
2. You can't touch* your elbow with your nose.		
3. You can't see the Eiffel Tower in London.		
4. Cats can't swim.		
5. I can spell the word 'favourite'. *(Well, can YOU?)*		

* touch: *berühren*

The modal verb "can" (2)

Add "can" or "can't". *Ergänze „can" oder „can't".*

Example: Susan ___*can*___ dance.

1. You ______________ write a letter with a rubber.
2. A teacher ______________ give you homework.
3. You ______________ go skiing in winter.
4. Where are you? I ______________ see you.
5. You ______________ eat this cheese. It's too old.
6. I ______________ stand mice. They are horrible.
7. ______________ you help me, please?
8. ______________ you say it again, please?
9. I ______________ write this word. ______________ you spell it, please?

The verb "have got" (1)

Add "have got" or "has got".
Ergänze „have got" oder „has got".

Example: Charlie *has got* glue in his school bag.

1. Caroline ____________________ many friends.
2. Emma and Gillian ____________________ new pencil cases.
3. Rajiv is not very good at maths. So he _______________ extra maths lessons.
4. Their dream classroom _______________ sofas and armchairs.
5. "Mr Graham, I ____________________ my textbook with me, but not my workbook." –

   "Maybe you ____________________ it in your school bag. Look again."

The verb "have got" (2)

What pets have they got?
Wem gehört welches Tier?

Example: *Debbie has got a bird.*

1. Mrs Pepper ____________________

   ____

2. Jo ____________________

   ____

   ____

3. Mr and Mrs Smith ____________________

   ____

   ____

4. Mike ____________________

   ____

   ____

5. Amy ____________________

   ____

   ____

The verb "have got" (3)

Fill in the right form of "have got".
Trage die richtige Form von „have got" ein.

Example: "*Have* you *got* a ticket for the game?" – "No, I *haven't got* a ticket."

1. "__________ they ________ a computer?" – "No, they ________________________ a computer."

2. "__________ she ________ a car?" – "Yes, she ________________________ a car."

3. "__________ you ________ a pen for me?" – "Yes, ________________________ a pen."

4. "__________ he ________ a new watch?" – "No, ________________________ a new watch."

The verb "have got" (4)

Write negative sentences with "have got".
Bilde verneinte Sätze mit „have got".

Example: I can't write the text. *(no pen)*

I haven't got a pen.

1. Emma can't read the text. *(no textbook)*

____

2. We can't do the maths exercise. *(no calculators)*

____

3. David can't sharpen his pencils. *(no pencil sharpener)*

____

4. I don't know when the geography lesson is. *(no timetable)*

____

5. Rajiv can't come. *(no time)*

____

6. Sorry, you can't listen to an English song in this lesson. *(no CD)*

____

The verb "have got" (5)

What have you got?
Ask questions and give short answers.
Schreibe über dich selbst.
Stelle Fragen und gib Kurzantworten darauf.

Example: You/mouse/in your house?

"Have you got a mouse in your house?" –

"Yes, I have."/"No, I haven't."

1. You/a TV/in your bedroom? ______

______

2. You/posters/on the walls of your bedroom? ______

______

3. Your family/a swimming pool/in the garden?

______

______

______

______

4. Your grandma/a hobby? ______

______

5. Your father/long hair? ______

______

6. Your mother/blue eyes? ______

______

7. You/any brothers or sisters? ______

______

Imperative (1)

"Don't do this, don't do that!"
What does the teacher say? Make sentences. Choose the verbs from the box.
Was sagt der Lehrer? Bilde Sätze mit den Verben aus dem Kasten.

~~do~~ • play • write • listen to • dance

Example: … your homework in class: *Don't do your homework in class!*

1. … love letters in class: ______________________

2. … on the desks: ______________________

3. … games on your mobile phones: ______________________

4. … music in class: ______________________

Imperative (2)

What does Mr Graham say? Look at the picture and write three sentences.
Was sagt Mr Graham? Schau dir das Bild an und schreibe drei Sätze.

Example:

Don't write on the blackboard, please.
Don't open the window!
Sit down, please. …

1. ______________________

2. ______________________

3. ______________________

Possessive determiners (1)

Complete the lists with the right possessive determiners and personal pronouns.
Vervollständige die Listen mit den passenden Possessivpronomen und Personalpronomen.

Personal pronoun	Possessive determiner
I	*my*
you	
we	
she	
he	
it	
you *(plural)*	
they	

Possessive determiner	Personal pronoun
his	*he*
our	
their	
your	
its	
my	
her	
your *(plural)*	

Possessive determiners (2)

Fill in the right possessive determiner.
Trage das passende Possessivpronomen ein.

Example:

David, have you got <u>your</u> homework?

1. Gillian and Emma, where are _______________ timetables?
2. We want to email David. Have you got _______________ email address?
3. David and I can't wash _______________ hands. There is no water.
4. Do you think that Rajiv and Caroline are happy at _______________ school?
5. We can't do _______________ homework because we don't understand it.
6. The pupils can't eat _______________ sandwiches in class.
7. I want to phone Gillian. Have you got _______________ telephone number?
8. Mr and Mrs Graham live in London. But _______________ son lives in America.

Personal pronoun or possessive determiner?

Mrs Scott and her friends

Fill in the right personal pronoun or possessive determiner.
Trage das richtige Personalpronomen oder Possessivpronomen ein.

Hello, ___I___ am Carol Scott. ________ am from Manchester and ________ have got many friends. ________ best friend is Ray. ________ likes reading and ________ has got many books. ________ likes cooking, too and ________ kitchen is very big. Ray is very big, too. Ray has got a funny dog. ________ name is Karen and ________ can do a lot of tricks. My friend Tracy has got a very nice house. ________ likes flowers. ________ two hamsters like to play in the garden. Sometimes ________ eat the flowers in Tracy's garden. Then ________ puts the hamsters back into ________ box. How are ________? Have ________ got pets, too? Are ________ nice?

Mr Pendlebury and his friends

Fill in the right personal pronoun or possessive determiner.
Trage das richtige Personalpronomen oder Possessivpronomen ein.

Hello, ___my___ name is Pendlebury, Jonathan Pendlebury. ________ am from London and ________ have got many friends. ________ best friend is Carla Peel. ________ is 76 years old, but ________ is very fit. ________ hobby is karate and ________ is very strong. Don't get in ________ way, or ________ will be in trouble. But don't worry, ________ is very nice. Carla has got an old goldfish. ________ name is Goldie. ________ doesn't talk so much, but ________ is a good swimmer. Gregory is another good friend. ________ is very funny and very, very tall, and ________ hands are very big. ________ plays basketball and ________ team is very good. Gregory and I play in a band. ________ plays the piano and ________ play the guitar. ________ often play at parties. The people like ________ and ________ dance to it. ________ is great. ________ love it. Now, what is ________ name? Where are ________ from? Have ________ got a hobby? What about ________ friends? Do ________ like music? Have ________ got hobbies? What about ________ pets? Do ________ like animals?

Questions with question words (1)

Match the questions with the answers.
Ordne die Fragen den Antworten zu.

1. Carl is at home.
2. My father can do magic tricks.
3. I can do the shopping.
4. This is my aunt.
5. We can't do this exercise.

a) Who is she?
b) Who can do it?
c) What can he do?
d) Why can't you (do it)?
e) Where is he?

Questions with question words (2)

Put in the right question word.
Setze das richtige Fragewort ein.

~~Where~~ • How • Why *(2x)* • What • Who • When

Example: *Where* is the party?

1. ______________________ many friends have you got?
2. ______________________ is this? Is she your new friend?
3. ______________________ don't you like the girl? I think she is nice.
4. ______________________ do you do on Friday evenings?
5. ______________________ does the party start?
6. ______________________ can't you come to my party?

Questions with question words (3)

Write down five questions.
Schreibe fünf Fragen.

How	have	they	help
Where	do	you	do
What	can	I	get up
When		we	live
			got

Example: *When do you get up?*

1. ______________________________?

2. ______________________________?

3. ______________________________?

4. ______________________________?

5. ______________________________?

Questions with question words (4)

Make questions which match the answers.
Bilde die Fragen zu den Antworten.

Example: My favourite colour is green. – *What is your favourite colour?*

1. We can play together on Thursday. –
______________________________?

2. I'm fine, thanks for asking. –
______________________________?

3. It's not her book. It's his. –
______________________________?

4. Sarah doesn't talk to me because I like Nicole. –
______________________________?

Prepositions (1)

Gillian and David are visiting Grandma Collins. They want to play a little trick on her. They have got ten mice (toys, of course). Read the text below and draw in the mice.
Gillian und David besuchen Oma Collins. Sie wollen ihr einen Streich spielen. Sie haben zehn Mäuse (natürlich Spielzeugmäuse). Lies den unten stehenden Text und zeichne die Mäuse ein.

Gillian: OK, let's put the blue mouse under the table, next to the remote control.
David: Good idea. And the black mouse goes into the cup, left of the teapot.
Gillian: Now, where can we put the red mouse?
David: How about the clock? Let's put it on the clock.
Gillian: And the orange mouse goes behind the TV magazine.
David: Good, now the green mouse goes behind the white bag.
Gillian: And the brown mouse goes right in front of it.
David: Brilliant. The purple mouse can go under the carpet.
Gillian: I don't know. I think we can put it under the table on the right.
David: OK. So what do we do with the yellow mouse?
Gillian: I've got it. The yellow mouse goes on the shelf, between the hippo and the elephant.
David: Now what about the grey mouse? Let's put it on the table, next to the flowers.
Gillian: Have we got them all?
David: No, we haven't. Look, here is the pink mouse.
Gillian: Let's put it on the chair.
David: The chair behind the flowers, in front of the window?
Gillian: No, the chair next to the telephone.
David: Good. Now I hope that Grandma doesn't get a shock.
Gillian: Oh no. That's no problem. She will find it funny.

Prepositions (2)

Fill in the right preposition.
Trage die richtige Präposition ein.

Example: Steven has got many pencils

_*on*_ his desk.

1. There are many posters ________________ elephants and football players ________________ the walls.
2. Let's paint your room ________________ Saturday ________________ nine o'clock.
3. You must ask dad ________________ the colour. We can't paint my room pink or black.
4. Diane is very interested ________________ Tommy's new bedroom.
5. Brad's room is a mess. So his mum tells him to tidy ________________ his room.

Prepositions (3)

Put the following expressions into English.
Übersetze die folgenden Wendungen ins Englische.

Example: neben dem Tisch: *next to the table*

1. auf dem Sofa: ______________________________
2. im Kleiderschrank: ______________________________
3. zwischen den Stühlen: ______________________________
4. über dem Bett: ______________________________
5. gegenüber dem Regal: ______________________________
6. unter dem Teppich: ______________________________
7. hinter dem Telefon: ______________________________
8. vor dem Fenster: ______________________________

Simple present (1)

Write down the simple present forms. Then find them in the grid.
Schreibe die Verben im simple present auf. Finde sie dann im Gitter.

Example: go: *she goes* ____________

1. watch: *she* ____________
2. do: *he* ____________
3. learn: *she* ____________
4. wash: *we* ____________
5. see: *he* ____________
6. make: *you* ____________
7. tidy: *he* ____________
8. think: *they* ____________
9. dance: *she* ____________
10. speak: *he* ____________

D	L	E	A	R	N	S	M
W	A	T	C	H	E	S	A
T	O	R	W	I	K	S	K
U	H	E	D	H	E	P	E
N	C	I	S	C	G	E	K
O	T	A	N	E	O	A	T
O	W	A	R	K	E	K	N
G	D	O	E	S	S	S	T

Simple present (2)

Put in the right verb in the right form.
Setze das richtige Verb in der richtigen Form ein.

Example: Charlie and David *play* football on Saturday afternoons.

~~play~~ • have • ask • go • cook • live • speak • make • get • clean • help

1. Caroline ____________ up at nine o'clock every morning.
2. Emma usually ____________ to the bathroom at eight o'clock.
3. On Saturdays we ____________ breakfast at ten o'clock.
4. Gillian's bike is very dirty. She never ____________ it.
5. Rajiv often ____________ his parents in the shop.
6. His parents sometimes ____________ him to tidy up his room.
7. My grandfather ____________ three languages: English, Hindi and French.
8. Mrs Pendlebury is very rich. She ____________ in a big house.
9. Caroline's dad ____________ the meals at weekends.
10. On Sundays Charlie ____________ tea for his mum and dad.

Simple present (3)

Put in the verbs in the correct form.
Setze die Verben in der richtigen Form ein.

A day in the life of Ghost Girl

It is (be) not easy to be a ghost. Ghosts always __________ (sleep) when we __________ (be) awake. And when night __________ (come) and everybody __________ (go) to bed, they __________ (wake) up. Jannet, a ghost girl, __________ (get) up at eleven o'clock. Her mum __________ (say) that she _____ (be) late. First Jannet __________ (go) to the bathroom and __________ (wash) her face. Then she __________ (have) breakfast with her family. They __________ (be) very quiet. But when it __________ (be) twelve, all the ghosts __________ (play) funny games. At one o'clock all the little ghosts __________ (go) to school. Jannet __________ (like) school because the teacher __________ (tell) her new tricks every day and he __________ (know) interesting stories. But sometimes Jannet __________ (dream) in class. Then the teacher __________ (say): "Jannet, you __________ (be) in dreamland. __________ (come) back into the classroom and __________ (sing) a ghost song with us." Mr Canterville __________ (think) that it __________ (be) very important to learn songs. Ghost school __________ (take) three hours. For the rest of the night, the ghosts __________ (put) on their make-up and __________ (try) to look terrible. Today Jannet __________ (want) to be a very old lady with two heads. "How __________ (be) you today", says head number one to head number two. "I __________ (be) fine, thank you." __________ (say) head number two. All the ghost children __________ (have) a lot of fun and when it __________ (be) time for bed, they __________ (be) very tired.

*through: *durch*

Negation of the simple present (1)

Add „don't" or „doesn't". *Ergänze „don't" oder „doesn't".*

Caroline's chaos

Example: Caroline *doesn't* tidy up her room.

1. Caroline ______________ feed her cat.
2. Caroline and her brother George ______________ make their beds.
3. Caroline's father ______________ help Caroline with her homework.
4. Caroline ______________ go shopping.
5. Caroline and her brother ______________ like the food their mum cooks for them.
6. Caroline's parents ______________ talk to their neighbours.
7. Caroline and George ______________ go to bed at nine.
8. Caroline's mum ______________ clean her bike.
9. George ______________ get to school on time. He is always late.
10. Caroline's father and mother ______________ make breakfast on Sunday.

Negation of the simple present (2)

Complete the following sentences with the words from the box. All the sentences are negative.
Vervollständige die folgenden Sätze mit den Wörtern aus dem Kasten. Alle Sätze sind verneint.

~~know~~ • play • like • put • need • have/have got *(2x)* • know • tidy up • make • go

Example: Gillian wants to wear her favourite shirt, but she *doesn't know* where it is.

1. George sometimes tidies up his room, but he ______________________ his bed.
2. We live in a nice flat, but we ______________________ a balcony.
3. Caroline and Gillian often listen to CDs, but they ______________________ computer games very often.
4. The walls of his room are white. He ______________________ that. He wants blue walls.
5. My family has only got one TV. And that's in the living room. So I ______________________ a TV in my room.
6. Emma has got a big wardrobe, but she ______________________ her clothes into it. She often leaves them on her bed.
7. Thanks for your help, but I ______________________ it. I can paint my room alone.
8. Oh no, the CDs ______________________ on this shelf. This shelf is for my books.
9. Sorry, I ______________________ where your dinosaur poster is. But perhaps dad knows.
10. Gillian's room is a mess, but she ______________________ it __________.

Simple present: questions (1)

Make questions with the verb in brackets.
Bilde Fragen mit dem Verb in der Klammer.

Example: *Does* your friend *watch* (watch) television a lot?

1. ____________ your mother ____________ (feed) the cat?
2. ____________ girls ____________ (like) shopping?
3. ____________ your dad ____________ (play) computer games?
4. ____________ you sometimes ____________ (clean) the kitchen?

Simple present: questions (2)

Write down seven questions. *Schreibe sieben Fragen auf.*

Does	you	feed	music	at the weekend
Do	Rajiv	go to	fish and chips	in the evening
	your mum and dad	enjoy	football matches	on Saturdays
	Charlie	tidy up	the goldfish	every morning
	her father	like	the flat	
	Gillian		parties	

Example: *Does Gillian go to parties (on Saturdays)?*

1. ____ ?
2. ____ ?
3. ____ ?
4. ____ ?
5. ____ ?
6. ____ ?
7. ____ ?

Simple present: questions and short answers

Make questions about you and your family and give short answers.
Bilde Fragen über dich und deine Familie und gib Kurzantworten.

Example: make breakfast sometimes *(you)*:

"Do you make breakfast sometimes?" –

"Yes, I do."/"No, I don't".

1. normally make your bed *(you)*: ______________________________

____

2. often drink milk for breakfast *(your mum)*: ______________________________

____

3. usually go to school by bus *(you)*: ______________________________

____

4. listen to music in the afternoon *(your brother/sister)*: ______________________________

____

5. pack your school bag before you go to bed *(you)*: ______________________________

____

6. often watch TV in the evening *(your brother/sister)*: ______________________________

____

7. usually read in bed *(your parents)*: ______________________________

____

8. sometimes have funny dreams at night *(you)*: ______________________________

____

Word order; adverbs of frequency (1)

Put the words in the right order. Then write down the sentences.
Bringe die Wörter in die richtige Reihenfolge. Schreibe dann die Sätze auf.

Example: [1] David [3] walks [2] often [4] the dog

David often walks the dog.

1. [ ] Gillian [ ] in the afternoon [ ] listens to music [ ] always

___

2. [ ] Emma [ ] plays tennis [ ] after school [ ] sometimes

___

3. [ ] Rajiv [ ] forgets [ ] his homework [ ] often

___

4. [ ] My father [ ] is [ ] home [ ] before 5 p.m. [ ] never

___

5. [ ] My friend Charlie [ ] can [ ] play [ ] computer games [ ] on his mother's computer [ ] usually

___

___

Word order; adverbs of frequency (2)

Correct or incorrect?
Correct the wrong sentences.
Richtig oder falsch?
Korrigiere die falschen Sätze.

Example: Charlie buys usually food on Saturday. *INCORRECT.*

Charlie usually buys food on Saturday.

1. David usually gets up at 6.30 a.m. ______

______

2. I drink often a cup of tea in the morning. ______

______

3. I help always my mother in the kitchen. ______

______

4. Our head teacher is never late for school. ______

______

5. In July our classroom is usually very hot. ______

______

6. After school we can play sometimes in the park. ______

______

7. Do you go always home at six? ______

______

8. Gillian reads a book often before she goes to bed. ______

______

s-genitive

Whose is it?
Name the objects and draw a line to the matching object.
Wem gehört es?
Benenne die Gegenstände und verbinde zum entsprechenden Gegenstand.

Example: Emma*'s watch*

1. Rajiv ____________________

2. Gillian ____________________

3. David ____________________

4. Caroline ____________________

5. Charlie ____________________

6. Emma ____________________

Look at the picture again. Can you name more objects?
Sieh dir das Bild noch einmal an. Kannst du weitere Gegenstände benennen?

Caroline's sunglasses, ____________________

____

____

Object pronouns (1)

Fill in the right pronoun. *Trage das richtige Pronomen ein.*

Example: I like Jack and he likes *me* ____ .

1. I love Jim and Jim loves ____________.

2. You love Jane and she loves ____________.

3. She loves John and John loves ____________.

4. He likes Jennifer and she likes ____________.

5. We love our dad and he loves ____________.

6. They like James and James likes ____________.

Object pronouns (2)

Tick ☑ the right pronoun.
Mache ein Häkchen ☑ beim richtigen Pronomen.

Example: Where is mum? Can you see …?

☐ she ☐ him ☐ us ☑ her

1. Dad, I don't know what to do. Can you play chess with …?

☐ I ☐ you ☐ my ☐ me

2. Great! Our mum has made wonderful sandwiches for ….

☐ he ☐ my ☐ their ☐ us

3. I don't like that boy and I don't want to play with ….

☐ he ☐ his ☐ him ☐ her

4. Have you got a new CD? Can we listen to …?

☐ its ☐ her ☐ it ☐ hers

Object pronouns (3)

Fill in the right pronoun.
Trage das richtige Pronomen ein.

Example: Where is Rajiv? I can't see *him*.

1. I like Gillian. I meet ______________ at school every day.
2. I don't know how to do this exercise. Can you help ______________?
3. Mrs Jones is not very friendly. I don't like ______________ very much.
4. Excuse me, Emma. Can you give ______________ that book there, please?
5. We gave ______________ our address and they gave ______________ theirs.

The modal verbs "must" and "have to" (1)

Complete the sentences. Use "have to" or "must".
Vervollständige die Sätze. Verwende dabei „have to" oder „must".

Example: Our mum says that we *have to clean/must clean* (clean) our teeth every day.

1. At my school you ______________________ (wear) a school uniform.
2. Dad says that I ______________________ (tidy up) the kitchen every week.
3. I ______________________ (do) homework every day.
4. It's my dog. I ______________________ (take) it for a walk every day.
5. My parents say that they ______________________ (work) a lot.

The modal verbs "must" and "have to" (2)

Make sentences with "don't/doesn't have to".
Bilde Sätze mit „don't/doesn't have to".

Example: Why do you get up so early?

You don't have to get up so early.

1. Why do you always talk to him?

____

2. Why do you give them all your money?

____

3. Why does he want to go out?

____

4. Why do they work so hard?

____

5. Why does she want to clean our car?

____

The modal verbs "must" and "have to" (3)

Complete the sentences with "must","have/has to" or "don't/doesn't have to" and the verbs from the box.
Vervollständige die Sätze mit "must",„have/has to" oder „don't/doesn't have to" und den Verben aus dem Kasten.

~~cook~~ • buy • clean • go • dance • write • take • do *(2x)* • be

Example: Can you help me in the kitchen, please?

We have guests tonight. So we *have to cook/must cook* dinner for eight people.

1. My mum is very busy today. That's why I ______ the shopping.
2. We live near the school, so we ______ the bus.
3. Dad's stomach is OK again. He ______ to the doctor's.
4. "Sorry, I can't find your CD." – "Then you ______ me a new one."
5. There is no school tomorrow. So I ______ my homework right now.
6. Sandra's friends are coming over to her place. So she ______ her room.
7. "I don't like dancing" – "That's alright. You ______ at our party."
8. She wants to send the letter in three weeks, so she ______ it now.
9. Don't worry! The pupils in your new class are all very nice. You ______ nervous.

Present progressive (1)

Fill in the correct form of "be".
Trage die richtige Form von „be" ein.

Example: Excuse me, you *are* walking the wrong way.

1. She __________ eating an apple.
2. I __________ going over to Caroline's house.
3. Oh no, it __________ raining again.
4. We __________ selling our old bikes.
5. They __________ walking past our shop.
6. Look, he __________ giving him the money.
7. __________ you looking at me?
8. OK, I __________ listening to you.

Present progressive (2)

What are these people doing?
Make sentences. Use the present progressive.
Was machen diese Leute gerade?
Bilde Sätze und verwende dabei das present progressive.

Example: My uncle/do/a magic trick:

My uncle is doing a magic trick.

1. Charlie/read/email: ______________________________
2. Rajiv/walk/to Camden Lock Market: ______________________________
3. We/look/at a cool poster: ______________________________
4. You/eat/my sandwich: ______________________________
5. I/look for/birthday presents: ______________________________
6. David/sit/in the kitchen: ______________________________
7. They/listen/to Caroline's new CD: ______________________________
8. I/dance/with my girlfriend: ______________________________
9. My parents/brush/their teeth: ______________________________
10. Her friend/watch/TV: ______________________________

Present progressive (3)

Make sentences. (Some have to be negative.)
Use the verbs from the box in the present progressive.
Bilde Sätze. (Manche müssen verneint werden.)
Verwende dazu die Verben aus dem Kasten im present progressive.

~~answer~~ • do *(2x)* • read • listen • open • dream • talk • ~~play~~ • watch • think • sit • check

Example: "At the moment, Gillian _*is answering*_ the phone.

She _*isn't playing*_ with the cat."

1. "What are you doing?" – "I ______________________ a book. Can't you see that?"
2. "Is that the new girl over there?" – "Yes, she ______________________ next to David. I think she likes him."
3. "Is Caroline in?" – "Yes, she is in her room. I think she ______________________ her emails."
4. "Is Charlie angry with Emma? He ______________________ to her."
5. "What are you doing with the cards?" – "I ______________________ a magic trick."
6. "Are your parents in bed already?" – "No, they ______________________ TV."
7. "What's that noise from the kitchen?" – "I ______________________ the fridge. I'm hungry."
8. "No, Mr Graham. I ______________________ in class. I ______________________ about your question."

9. "Where is that music coming from?" – "Oh, that's Caroline and Gillian. They ______________________ to a new CD. And that tells me that they ______________________ their homework."

Present progressive: questions

Make questions. Use the present progressive.
Bilde Fragen. Verwende dabei das present progressive.

Example:

What/you/cook?

What are you cooking?

1. Where/you/go?
2. What/you/do?
3. Why/he/go home?
4. She/answer/the phone?
5. They/dance/with their friends?
6. I/eat/your pizza?
7. What/you/look at?
8. Where/she/sleep?
9. She/sleep/in my bed?
10. Why/we/sit/in the kitchen?

Present progressive: questions and short answers

Make questions and answers in the present progressive.
Bilde Fragen und Antworten im present progressive.

Example: Charlie/make/coffee? – No. He/make/tea

"Is Charlie making coffee?" – "No, he isn't. He is making tea."

1. David/talk/to Gillian? – No. David/talk/to Rajiv

2. They/sleep/in her room? – Yes

3. You/eat/a pizza? – No. I/eat/kebab

4. Caroline/have/a good time? – Yes

5. Emma/cook/dinner? – No. She/talk to/her friends

6. You/watch/TV? – No. I/wash up/the plates

Simple present or present progressive? (1)

Check the underlined verbs. Are they correct?
If not, write down the right form.
Überprüfe die unterstrichenen Verben. Sind sie korrekt?
Schreibe die richtige Form auf, falls nicht.

	correct	incorrect	
Example: David is in the bathroom. He <u>brushes</u> his teeth right now.		X	*is brushing*
1. "Come on, we must go." – "OK, <u>I'm coming</u>".			
2. "Can you see those two boys?" – "What <u>do they do</u>?"			
3. Look. Caroline <u>is eating</u> my apple.			
4. She is in a new basketball team. They <u>have</u> matches every weekend.			
5. We <u>are</u> often <u>going</u> to school by bus.			
6. <u>I don't know</u> anybody at this party.			
7. We <u>are</u> always <u>having</u> a warm meal in the evening.			
8. I don't believe it! Look, Jane <u>drinks</u> from my bottle.			
9. My dad is always cool. He <u>is</u> never <u>shouting</u> at me.			
10. Be careful. This dog is dangerous. It <u>bites</u>.			

Simple present or present progressive? (2)

Cross out the part of the sentence that doesn't fit.
Streiche den falschen Teil des Satzes durch.

Example: We can't go out now. It ~~rains~~ / is raining.

1. Where is your sister? – In the kitchen. She makes / is making a meal.
2. Can you speak more slowly? I don't understand / am not understanding you.
3. My father is usually coming / usually comes home at 5.30 p.m.
4. I always read / am always reading before I go to bed.
5. Excuse me. Do you speak / Are you speaking German?

Simple present or present progressive? (3)

Make sentences.
Use the simple present or the present progressive.
Bilde Sätze.
Verwende dabei simple present oder present progressive.

Example: Look over there! David and Charlie/play/football.

David and Charlie are playing football.

1. Where is Caroline? – She's in her room. She/play/a new computer game.

____

2. Where is Rajiv? – I/not/know.

____

3. Excuse me, sir. You/speak/English?

____

4. We must go. You/come?

____

5. Would you like some lemonade, Emma? – No, thanks! I/not like/lemonade.

____

Simple present or present progressive? (4)

How do you say it in English? *Wie sage ich es auf Englisch?*

Example: Du telefonierst mit deinem Freund. Du fragst ihn, ob er gerade einen Apfel isst.

Are you eating an apple? ______________________________

1. Jemand ist gerade in deinem Zimmer. Du fragst, was er dort tut.

____

2. Du fragst jemanden, was er normalerweise am Sonntag macht.

____

3. Du möchtest sagen, dass dein Bruder gerade Gitarre spielt.

____

4. Du teilst mit, dass deine Schwester jeden Tag Fußball spielt.

____

5. Sage jemandem, dass es gerade regnet.

____

Demonstrative pronouns

Add "this", "that", "these" or "those". *Ergänze „this", „that", „these" oder „those".*

Example: Hi! ___*This*___ is Caroline, a good friend of mine.

1. Look at ______________ house over there. It's beautiful, isn't it?
2. Excuse me, is ______________ your watch?
3. How much are ______________ posters over there?
4. Oh dear, ______________ car is too expensive. We must buy a different one.
5. I really like ______________ poster in Rajiv's room. It's cool.
6. Sorry I forgot your CD. – ______________'s OK. Don't worry.
7. Do you know ______________ boys over there in the corner?
8. Are __________ your keys?

Simple past (1)

Fill in the correct simple past form of "be".
Trage die richtige Form von "be" im simple past ein.

In the pet shop

Last year we *were* in a pet shop. We wanted to buy a dog, but in the end we didn't. The dog that I liked __________ too big and too expensive. The dog's ears __________ pink. They __________ funny. The dog __________ very friendly, but my friend Emma didn't like it very much. She __________ a bit scared. The shop assistant __________ nice. She __________ very young. Her parents __________ from Italy. She __________ sorry that we didn't buy the dog. And so __________ I.

Simple past (2)

Put in the right verb from the box. Use the simple past.
Setze das richtige Verb aus dem Kasten im simple past ein.

> ~~escape~~ • take • eat • buy • call • find • go • drive • ~~catch~~ • like • meet • be • get • ask • have

Example: Last week, a tiger *escaped* from the zoo.
But the police *caught* it some hours later.

1. I ______________ many birthday presents. I really ______________ that.
2. My father ______________ us to my grandma's house and we ______________ a great party with all the family.
3. Yesterday, Owen ______________ Hannah on the phone.
4. My brother ______________ a hamster in the playground. He ______________ it home.
5. At school, my sister ______________ all my sandwiches. So I ______________ to the cafeteria and ______________ fish and chips.
6. Last week, I ______________ Jessica in town. She ______________ me to give you this note.

Negation of the simple past (1)

Complete the sentences.
Fill in the negative form of the verb.
Vervollständige die Sätze.
Trage dazu das Verb in der verneinten Form ein.

Example: The tiger wanted to run away from the zoo,

but it *didn't want* to kill anyone.

1. His parents bought a cat, but they ____________________ a dog.
2. We talked about our pets, but we ____________________ about our hobbies.
3. We saw the little sheep, but we ____________________ the sheepdog.
4. Grandma took a nice photo of us, but she ____________________ a photo of the animals.
5. He gave the dog something to eat, but he ____________________ him any water.
6. They played with their hamster on Tuesday, but they ____________________ with it on Wednesday.
7. I heard the dog when it came in, but I ____________________ mum.
8. The mice ate all the cheese, but they ____________________ our sausages.
9. We knew about the zoo's new elephant, but we ____________________ ____________________ about the new lions.
10. My sister thinks that the crocodile looked funny, but it ____________________ ____________________ funny to me.

Negation of the simple past (2)

Amy and Martin didn't do any of their jobs last week.
Now their parents are inspecting the flat. What do the parents say?
Amy und Martin haben in der letzten Woche ihre Aufgaben nicht erledigt.
Nun kontrollieren ihre Eltern die Wohnung. Was sagen die Eltern?

Monday	Tuesday	Wednesday	Thursday	Friday	Saturday	Sunday
clean the table	*throw out the old clothes*	*wipe the chairs*	*sweep behind the sofa*	*hoover the floor*	*tidy up the wardrobe*	*no jobs*

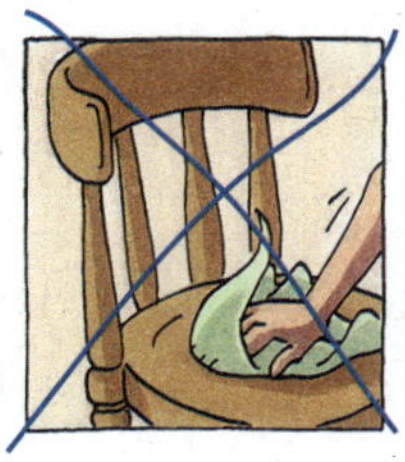

Example:

You didn't wipe the chairs on Wednesday.

1. ______________________________

____

2. ______________________________

____

3. ______________________________

____

4. ______________________________

____

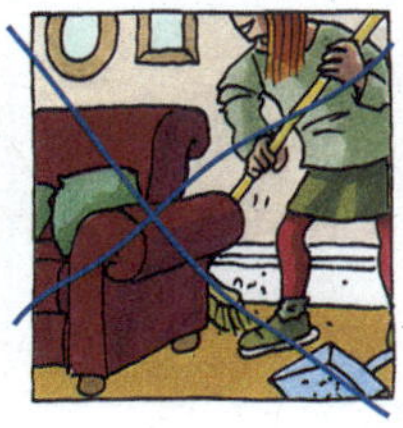

5. ______________________________

____

Simple past: questions (1)

Make questions. *Bilde Fragen.*

Did	he	set	your homework?
	you	make	the plants?
	she	do	shopping?
		go	the washing up?
		water	the table?
			the bed?

Example:

Did you do your homework?

3. ______________________

1. ______________________

4. ______________________

2. ______________________

5. ______________________

Simple past: questions (2)

Make questions in the simple past. *Bilde Fragen im simple past.*

Examples: When/you/buy/a new bike? *When did you buy a new bike?*

1. What/they/do/at five? ______________________
2. Where/you/go/yesterday? ______________________
3. Why/you/do/that? ______________________
4. Why/they/not/come back? ______________________
5. When/she/come home? ______________________
6. What/they/see? ______________________
7. Who/you/talk to? ______________________

Simple past: questions and short answers

Make questions and answers in the simple past.
Bilde Fragen und Antworten im simple past.

Example: The tiger/eat/a tourist? – No. It/eat/a sandwich

"Did the tiger eat a tourist?" –

"No, it didn't. It ate a sandwich."

1. The tiger/swim/in the swimming pool? – No. It/swim/in the canal

2. You/forget/to feed the dog? – No. But/I/forget/to feed the goldfish

3. They/wash up/the dirty cups? – Yes

4. You/pull/a big fish out of the water? – No. I/only/pull/an old boot out of the water

5. Carla/help/Grandfather/with the shopping? – Yes

6. James/be/near the river yesterday? – No. But/he/be/in the park

7. The ghosts/live/in your house? –
   No. They/live/in the hotel next to our house

Simple past (revision)

Put in the verbs in the correct form.
Setze die Verben in der richtigen Form ein.

A story from the life of Spooky Boy

Yesterday, Spooky Boy got (get) up at 11.45 p.m. He ______ (be) late for school, so Spooky Boy ______ (not/go) to the bathroom and ______ (not/wash) his face. He ______ (have) a very quick breakfast with his family. First they ______ (not/say) anything. Then his mother ______ (want) to know: "______ you ______ (pack) your schoolbag yesterday?" – "Yes, I did, mum". "And ______ you ______ (do) your homework?" – "No, I didn't. We ______ (not/have to) do any homework!"

At midnight all the little ghosts ______ (go) to ghost school. Yesterday they ______ (learn) how to transform* into a wild dog. Spooky Boy ______ (like) the lesson, but he ______ (make) a big mistake. He ______ (not/become) a wild dog. He ______ (become) a little mouse. All the wild dogs ______ (want) to eat him and he ______ (be) in big trouble. But his teacher ______ (help) him.

Then they ______ (learn) how to dance a really terrible ghost dance. But Spooky Boy soon ______ (forget) how the steps** ______ (go). So the other ghost kids ______ (laugh) at him and ______ (say): "______ you ______ (see) him? He ______ (not/understand) anything."

But then they ______ (have) a ghost sports lesson. And Spooky Boy ______ (be) really good. Nobody ______ (fly) as fast as he did. Now Spooky Boy ______ (feel) great and when he ______ (come) home, he ______ (tell) his parents all about it. And when he ______ (fall) asleep in the morning, he ______ (dream) that he had won the ghost school flying championship.

*transform: *sich verwandeln*
**steps *hier: Schritte*

Lösungen

S. 5: Nouns: singular and plural (1): 1. shoes; 2. sausages; 3. watches; 4. days; 5. teeth; 6. hobbies; 7. pets; 8. men
S. 5: Nouns: singular and plural (2): 1 earrings; 2. stories; 3. glasses; 4. shelves; 5. lives; 6. feet
S. 6: Nouns: singular and plural; "there is"/"there are": *individuelle Lösungen*
S. 6: The article: 1. a; 2. an; 3. a; 4. an; 5. an; 6. an, an
S. 7: Personal pronouns (1): he: Mr Rice, a boy, (a little dog); she: Emma, Grandma Simpson, (a cat); it: a poster, a football, a little dog, a fish, a cat; they: CDs, David and Hoover; friends
S. 8: Personal pronouns (2): 1. We; 2. He; 3. it; 4. She; 5. it; 6. you; 7. it; 8. They; 9. It; 10. they 11. He; 12. They
S. 9: Personal pronouns (3): (1) He; (2) They; (3) He; (4) He; (5) They; (6) he; (7) She; (8) It; (9) he; (10) She/He; (11) you; (12) you; (13) He/It; (14) I; (15) it; (16) I; (17) It; (18) It; (19) They; (20) He; (21) you; (22) you; (23) I; (24) They; (25) you; (26) she; (27) I; (28) He; (29) It; (30) You; (31) you; (32) it
S. 10: The modal verb "can" (1): 1. false; 2. true; 3. true; 4. false *(but they don't like water)*; 5. *individuelle Lösung*
S. 10: The modal verb "can" (2): 1. can't; 2. can; 3. can; 4. can't; 5. can't; 6. can't; 7. Can; 8. Can; 9. can't; Can
S. 11: The verb "have got" (1): 1. has got; 2. have got; 3. has got; 4. has got; 5. have got, have got
S. 11: The verb "have got" (2): 1. Mrs Pepper has got a dog.; 2. Jo has got a rabbit.; 3. Mr and Mrs Smith have got a fish.; 4. Mike has got a cat.; 5. Amy has got a hedgehog.
S. 12: The verb "have got" (3): 1. Have ... got, haven't got; 2. Has ... got, has got; 3. Have ... got, I have got; 4. Has ... got, he hasn't got
S. 12: The verb "have got" (4): 1. She hasn't got a textbook.; 2. We haven't got (our) calculators.; 3. He hasn't got a pencil sharpener.; 4. I haven't got a timetable.; 5. He hasn't got time.; 6. You/We/I haven't got a CD.
S. 13: The verb "have got" (5): 1. Have you got a TV in your bedroom? – Yes, I have./No, I haven't.; 2. Have you got posters on the walls of your bedroom? – Yes, I have./No, I haven't.; 3. Has your family got a swimming pool in the garden? – Yes, they have./No, they haven't. *oder:* Yes, it has./No, it hasn't.; 4. Has your grandma got a hobby? – Yes, she has./No, she hasn't.; 5. Has your father got long hair? – Yes, he has./No, he hasn't.; 6. Has your mother got blue eyes? – Yes, she has./No, she hasn't.; 7. Have you got any brothers or sisters? – Yes, I have./No, I haven't.
S. 14: Imperative (1): 1. Don't write love letters in class. 2. Don't dance on the desks. 3. Don't play games on your mobile phones. 4. Don't listen to music in class.
S. 14: Imperative (2): *individuelle Lösungen, z. B.* Don't write on the blackboard!; Don't walk around, please.; Go away from the window; Don't do your homework in class!; Be quiet, please. ...
S. 15: Possessive determiners (1): *possessive determiners:* your, our, her, his, its; your; their; *personal pronouns:* we; they; you; it; I; she; you
S. 16: Possessive determiners (2): 1. your; 2. his; 3. our; 4. their; 5. our; 6. their; 7. her; 8. their
S. 17: Personal pronoun or possessive determiner?: *Text 1, Mrs Scott:* I; I; My; He; he; He; his; Its; it; She; Her; they; she; their; you; you; they
Text 2, Mr Pendlebury: I; I; My; She; she; Her; she; her; you; she; Its; It; it; He; his; He; his; He; I; We; our; they; It; I/We; your; you; you; your; they; they; their; they
S. 18: Questions with question words (1): 1-e); 2-c); 3-b); 4-a); 5-d)
S. 18: Questions with question words (2): 1. How; 2. Who; 3. Why; 4. What; 5. When; 6. Why
S. 19: Questions with question words (3): *individuelle Lösungen, z. B.* Where do they live?; How can I help?; What can we do?; What have you got?; How do you do?; Where can they live?; ...
S. 19: Questions with question words (4): 1. When can we play together?; 2. How are you?; 3. Whose book is this?; 4. Why doesn't she talk to you?
S. 20: Prepositions (1): *hier sollten die Mäuse eingezeichnet sein: blaue Maus unterm Tisch neben der Fernbedienung; schwarze Maus in der Tasse links vom Teekessel; rote Maus auf der Uhr; orange Maus hinter der Fernsehzeitschrift; grüne Maus hinter der weißen Tasche; braune Maus vor der weißen Tasche; lila Maus unter dem Tisch rechts; gelbe Maus auf dem Regal zwischen Nilpferd und Elefant; graue Maus auf dem selben Tische neben den Blumen; rosa Maus auf dem Stuhl neben dem Telefon*
S. 21: Prepositions (2): 1. of, on; 2. on, at; 3. about; 4. in; 5. up
S. 21: Prepositions (3): 1. on the sofa; 2. in the wardrobe; 3. between the chairs; 4. above/over the bed; 5. opposite the shelf; 6. under the carpet;

7. behind the telephone; 8. in front of the window
S. 22: Simple present (1): 1. watches; 2. does; 3. learns; 4. wash; 5. sees; 6. make; 7. tidies; 8. think; 9. dances; 10. speaks
S. 22: Simple present (2): 1. gets; 2. goes; 3. have; 4. cleans; 5. helps; 6. ask; 7. speaks; 8. lives; 9. cooks; 10. makes
S. 23: Simple present (3): *Zeile 1:* sleep; *Z.2:* are; comes; *Z.3:* goes; wake; *Z.4:* gets; *Z.5:* says; is; goes; *Z.6:* washes; has; *Z.7:* are; *Z.8:* is; play; *Z.9:* go; *Z.10:* likes; tells; *Z.11:* knows; *Z.12:* dreams; says; *Z.13:* are; Come; *Z.14:* sing; *Z.15:* thinks; is; *Z.16:* takes; *Z.17:* put; try; *Z.18:* wants; *Z.19:* are; *Z.20:* am; says; *Z.21:* have; is; *Z.22:* are
S. 24: Negation of the simple present (1): 1. doesn't; 2. don't; 3. doesn't; 4. doesn't; 5. don't; 6. don't; 7. don't; 8. doesn't; 9. doesn't; 10. don't
S. 25: Negation of the simple present (2): 1. doesn't make; 2. haven't got/don't have; 3. don't play; 4. doesn't like; 5. haven't got/don't have; 6. doesn't put; 7. don't need; 8. don't go; 9. don't know; 10. doesn't tidy ... up;
S. 26: Simple present: questions (1): 1. Does ... feed; 2. Do ... like; 3. Does ... play; 4. Do ... clean
S. 26: Simple present: questions (2): *individuelle Lösungen, z. B.* Do your mum and dad feed the goldfish at the weekend?; Does her father enjoy parties?; Does Rajiv like music?; Does Charlie go to football matches on Saturdays?; Does Gillian like fish and chips in the evening?; Do you tidy up the flat every morning?; ...
S. 27: Simple present: questions and short answers: 1. Do you normally make your bed? – Yes, I do./No, I don't.; 2. Does your mum often drink milk for breakfast? – Yes, she does./No, she doesn't.; 3. Do you usually go to school by bus? – Yes, I do./ No, I don't.; 4. Does your sister (brother) listen to music in the afternoon? – Yes, she (he) does./No, she (he) doesn't.; 5. Do you pack your school bag before you go to bed? – Yes, I do./No, I don't.; 6. Does your brother (sister) often watch TV in the evening? – Yes, he (she) does./No, he (she) doesn't.; 7. Do your parents usually read in bed? – Yes, they do./No, they don't.; 8. Do you sometimes have funny dreams at night? – Yes, I do./No, I don't.
S. 28: Word order; adverbs of frequency (1): 1. Gillian always listens to music in the afternoon.; 2. Emma sometimes plays tennis after school.; 3. Rajiv often forgets his homework.; 4. My father is never home before 5 p.m.; 5. My friend Charlie can usually play computer games on his mother's computer.
S. 29: Word order; adverbs of frequency (2): 1. correct; 2. incorrect: I often drink a ...; 3. incorrect: I always help my mother ...; 4. correct; 5. correct; 6. incorrect: After school we can sometimes play...; 7. incorrect: Do you always go home at six?; 8. incorrect: Gilliam often reads a book ...
S. 30: s-genitive: *verschiedene Antworten sind möglich, z. B.* 1. Rajiv's guitar; 2. Gillian's camera; 3. David's dog; 4. Caroline's mobile; 5. Charlie's football; 6. Emma's bottle; *weitere mögliche Antworten:* Gillian's bag, Caroline's earring, David's baseball cap; Emma's skirt, Rajiv's nose, Emma's mp3 player, Caroline's boots, ...
S. 30: Object pronouns (1): 1. me; 2. you; 3. her; 4. him; 5. us; 6. them
S. 31: Object pronouns (2): 1. me; 2. us; 3. him; 4. it
S. 31: Object pronouns (3): 1. her; 2. me; 3. her; 4. me; 5. them, us
S. 32: The modal verbs "must" and "have to" (1): 1. have to wear/must wear; 2. have to tidy up/must tidy up; 3. have to do/must do; 4. have to take/must take; 5. have to work/must work
S. 32: The modal verbs "must" and "have to" (2): 1.You don't have to talk to him.; 2. You don't have to give them all your money.; 3. He doesn't have to go out.; 4. They don't have to work so hard.; 5. She doesn't have to clean our car.
S. 33: The modal verbs "must" and "have to" (3): 1. have to do/must do; 2. don't have to take; 3. doesn't have to go; 4. must buy/have to buy; 5. don't have to do; 6. has to clean/must clean; 7. don't have to dance; 8. doesn't have to write; 9. don't have to be
S. 34: Present progressive (1): 1. is; 2. am; 3. is; 4. are; 5. are; 6. is; 7. Are; 8. am
S. 34: Present progressive (2): 1. Charlie is reading an email.; 2. Rajiv is walking to Camden Market.; 3. We are looking at a cool poster.; 4. You are eating my sandwich.; 5. I am looking for birthday presents.; 6. David is sitting in the kitchen.; 7. They are listening to Caroline's new CD.; 8. I am dancing with my girlfriend.; 9. My parents are brushing their teeth.; 10. Her friend is watching TV.
S. 35: Present progressive (3): 1. am reading; 2. is sitting; 3. is checking; 4. isn't talking; 5. am doing; 6. are watching; 7. am opening; 8. am not dreaming, am thinking; 9. are listening, aren't doing
S. 36: Present progressive: questions: 1. Where are you going?; 2. What are you doing?; 3. Why is he going home?; 4. Is she answering the phone?; 5. Are they dancing with their friends?; 6. Am I eating your pizza?; 7. What are you looking at?;